YOU ARE THE GIRL FOR THE JOB

DARING TO BELIEVE
THE GOD WHO CALLS YOU

Jess Connolly

STUDY GUIDE | SIX SESSIONS

ZONDERVAN®

ZONDERVAN

You Are the Girl for the Job Study Guide
Copyright © 2019 by Jess Connolly

ISBN 978-0-310-09419-7 (softcover)
ISBN 978-0-310-09422-7 (ebook)

Requests for information should be addressed to:
Zondervan, 3900 Sparks Dr. SE, Grand Rapids, Michigan 49546

Published in association with literary agent Jenni Burke of D.C. Jacobson & Associates
LLC, an Author Management Company, www.dcjacobson.com

Designer: Hannah Warren
Photographer: John Hillin Photography

First Printing August 2019 / Printed in the United States of America

CONTENTS

NOTE FROM JESS

Friend, I want to tell you something about the front cover of the study guide, book, and video. It was very intentional, and it actually had a lot more to do with a revelation from God than you might think.

As you're doing this Bible study you're going to come face to face with this truth: I often struggle to believe that I'm the girl for the job too. I press into the message with you, alongside you, because the alternative is doubting God, His power, and His capacity in our lives.

When my friends were praying and dreaming about what the book cover needed to communicate, I realized it was super important that whoever reads and digs into this message doesn't hear *me* saying they're the girl for the job—it's important that they tell it to themselves. We have to learn so many lessons for ourselves or else they don't take root. Before we take a step further, it should be clear that by the time we're done, I want you to be able to tell yourself *you're* the girl for the job, not because it's a cute message but because it's the truth of God.

When you see the cover, I pray you will remember that this is *God's* message you're receiving, not a fluffy statement that some author is telling you casually.

HOW TO USE THIS GUIDE

GROUP SIZE

The *You Are the Girl for the Job* video study is designed to be experienced in a group setting, such as a Bible study, community group, or any other small group setting. To ensure everyone has enough time to participate in discussions after the video teaching, smaller groups of six to eight women are recommended.

MATERIALS NEEDED

Each participant will need her own copy of this study guide. For the most comprehensive personal experience of the material, an individual copy of the book *You Are the Girl for the Job* is encouraged. One copy (per group) of the DVD or the ability to view digital video sessions is required.

STUDY GUIDE

A schedule is included at the beginning of every session to help you plan and prepare for each group meeting as well as to see the personal study time planned for that session.

This study guide contains fill-in-the-blank spaces to follow along with the video teaching as well as margin room to take personal notes. Group discussion questions follow the video, as well as a weekly group exercise that deals with changing our language in order to change our culture.

You will have three days of personal study to do on your own between sessions. You can break it into smaller bits or do it all at once. The personal time exercises go in a pattern each week. On the first day, you'll let God speak to your heart and emotions regarding the topic of that session. On the second day, you'll engage your mind with some deeper biblical history and study. On the third day, you'll focus heavily on application and agreeing to God's Word with *your actions*. By the time you meet with your group again, whatever truth you've studied will be deeply implanted in your heart, your head, and your life.

Note: If you are unable to finish (or even start!) the between-sessions personal study, still attend the group study video session. We are all busy, and life happens. You are still wanted and welcome at the group even if you don't have your "homework" done.

Keep in mind that this is an opportunity to train yourself to see the world as God sees it. The videos, discussions, and personal studies are simply meant to kick-start your imagination in order to help you see how God is working through you already.

TIMING

The time notations next to each group section indicate either the actual video run time or the suggested time you can expect for discussion and activities. Each group meeting should be able to be completed in 60–90 minutes, depending on how much time you choose to allow for discussion.

LEADING A GROUP

Each group should appoint a leader who is responsible for starting the video and keeping track of time during discussions and activities. Leaders often find it useful to read the discussion questions in advance.

LET'S QUIT

SCHEDULE

Review this week's schedule as a group before opening your time together.

BEFORE THE GROUP MEETING	Read the introduction and chapters 1–3 in *You Are the Girl for the Job* book.*
IN YOUR GROUP	• Welcome from Jess • Set the Temperature (prayer) • Personal Heart Check-In • Watch the video teaching for Session 1 and take notes • Complete Discussion Questions • Change the Language/Change the Culture • My Prayer + Your Prayer
AT HOME	• Personal Study Day 1 (engage your heart with God's love) • Personal Study Day 2 (fill your head with God's truth) • Personal Study Day 3 (agree with abundance)
PREP FOR NEXT GROUP MEETING	Count the fruit of what God's done. Read chapters 4–6 in the *You Are the Girl for the Job* book.*

Reading through the book will enhance your experience of this study, but it is NOT required.

GROUP STUDY

WELCOME NOTE FROM JESS (2 MINUTES)

Leader, *read Note from Jess aloud to the group.*

Friends! I am so excited to be with you, to grow with you, over the next six weeks. There's no getting around it. I believe God is going to change each of us, change our lives, and change the world through this study. Here's how I know:

> For as the sky soars high above earth,
> so the way I work surpasses the way you work,
> and the way I think is beyond the way you think.
> Just as rain and snow descend from the skies
> and don't go back until they've watered the earth,
> Doing their work of making things grow and blossom,
> producing seed for farmers and food for the hungry,
> So will the words that come out of my mouth
> not come back empty-handed.
> They'll do the work I sent them to do,
> they'll complete the assignment I gave them.
>
> —Isaiah 55:9–11 MSG

We are the girls for the job because He is the one who starts and finishes the work in and through us. We can believe that He'll bring fruit in our lives because His Word does not come back empty-handed.

SET THE TEMPERATURE (2 MINUTES)

Pick someone to open the group in prayer before we do our personal heart check.

PERSONAL HEART CHECK (3 MINUTES)

Before we dig into this session's video, let's do a quick personal heart check. Take a minute or two to answer the following questions. You don't have to share these answers; this is just an opportunity for you to pause and get honest with yourself and God.

A. On a scale of 1–10 (1 = very little, 10 = significantly), mark how much you believe God can change your life and change the world through you?

1   2   3   4   5   6   7   8   9   10

B. How does the phrase "you are the girl for the job" make you feel? (Circle, underline, or highlight which option you resonate with most.)

SUSPICIOUS   DOUBTFUL   NEUTRAL   ENCOURAGED

C. How willing are you to be surprised by God this week? (Circle, underline, or highlight how you feel this week.)

WON'T HAPPEN   THAT SOUNDS NICE   TEACH ME, CHANGE ME, SURPRISE ME

VIDEO TEACHING (21 MINUTES)

Watch the Session 1 video. Fill in the blanks throughout the teaching if you'd like:

● God has call each of us to be his _____.

● God does not make _____.

● God's _____ will combat our _____.

- Ideal you is not nearly as _____ as _____ you.

- God is _____ He _____ He is.

- God is not going to stop _____ _____ OR _____ _____.

God is the hero. We are part of the rescue plan.

Take notes if you'd like:

Answer key: ambassadors, mistakes, capacity/inadequacy, strong/actual, who/says, showing up/walk away

GROUP DISCUSSION (30 MINUTES)

Leader, *read each question aloud to the group. Take turns/volunteers for any Scripture reading.*

1. What does "ideal you" look like? In a few words, describe her to the group—her state of mind, her movement through the day, her perspective, maybe her character traits and most defined attributes.

2. In what areas of life do you currently struggle to feel adequate? Discuss what you think is making you feel inadequate. Is it the standard you have set? A standard you perceive others to hold? Is your inadequacy backed up in Scripture anywhere?

3. Where do you find yourself asking God, "Why me?" Are there burdens you feel overwhelmed by? Are there circumstances you are being called to engage or deal with that challenge you or bring you out of your comfort zone? Is there something or someone you find yourself dealing with but don't feel equipped to handle?

4. What would change if you believed that God was going to bring you what you needed to accomplish whatever He has presented you? Would your attitude, your perspective, your willingness, your openness change? In what ways would you behave differently?

5. **Look up and read Hebrews 12:1–2 aloud.** Take turns sharing what you need to quit to fully embrace God's call on your life. What do you need to throw off that hinders and so easily entangles you? With what are you engaging that is keeping you from fixing your eyes on Jesus, from acknowledging the race marked out for you? (Ex.: being the best wife, being the most servant hearted, winning at life.)

CHANGE THE LANGUAGE, CHANGE THE CULTURE
(20 MINUTES)

When we change the language, we change the culture. When we put different words in our mouths, words that agree with God's character and capacity, things begin to shift not only in our lives but also in our communities.

Read Proverbs 18:21 aloud together.

Select one person to read a statement from the left column, and then have another person read the alternate statement in the right column. Talk about the difference you hear and feel in each change in the language. Discuss how these simple shifts in our language can effect change in our immediate culture. Commit to using language with one another that agrees with God's Word.

INSTEAD OF:	TRY THIS:
One day I'll get my junk together. (this reinforces an ideal-self that's never coming)	God has placed me in this season on purpose, with what I need to love and serve others.
Becky is the BEST mom. (this puts people on a pedestal and denotes that there is a competition)	Becky is being faithful to God's call on her life, and her example encourages me to do what God has called me to also!
I'm not sure why God picked me for this. (this doubts His intentional wisdom and power)	I know it's God's capacity that matters and it's such a privilege to use what I've got to serve Him!
I'm so overwhelmed and not sure how this is going to work out. (this speaks chaos into places where He already has a plan)	I can't wait to see how God works this out. It looks dark, but I know He's got this.

Keep telling each other that you're the girl for the job, because what's the alternative?

Keep reminding one another that He is mighty in each of you, because you get to, because He's placed you in each other's lives on purpose—for His glory and the good of others.

God is the hero. I am only a part of the rescue plan. I can quit trying to be the best, quit doubting my place in His plan of redemption, and start believing that He has placed me here on purpose. I *am* the girl for the job.

MY PRAYER + YOUR PRAYER (10 MINUTES)

Each week ask a volunteer to read the short prayer for the group, *but* because *you're the girl for the job*, each of you will also write a short prayer for yourself. Where are you asking God to meet you this week? What are you hoping will happen?

Father, I thank you for our new friends and our connection through Your Word. I ask this week that you'd help each of us to see potential defeat in our lives, to perceive it in places where we may have grown numb to the lies and condemning voices in our own heads. I ask that You would also give us eyes to see areas where we are striving, hiding, and pushing hard to be our ideal selves—instead of the women you've created us to be. I pray you give us the boldness and belief to quit trying to be heroes, and to begin trusting Your capacity and power in our lives. Amen.

Your turn:

_____

_____

_____

_____

_____

_____

UP NEXT

Leader, *before dismissing remind the group of what comes next.*

- Count the fruit of what God's done and write it down or share with someone.

_____

_____

_____

_____

- There are three days of personal study time to complete before we meet again.

- Read chapters 4–6 in *You Are the Girl for the Job* book if you are following along.

PERSONAL
STUDY

DAY ONE:
HEART

I find that so many heart issues that keep us from experiencing the fullness of God come from a lack of understanding about our relationship with Him: how we got it, how we experience it, and how we share it.

Let's read a little from Ephesians 2, The Message Version:

> Now God has us where he wants us, with all the time in this world and the next to shower grace and kindness upon us in Christ Jesus. Saving is all his idea, and all his work. All we do is trust him enough to let him do it. It's God's gift from start to finish! We don't play the major role. If we did, we'd probably go around bragging that we'd done the whole thing! No, we neither make nor save ourselves. God does both the making and saving. He creates each of us by Christ Jesus to join him in the work he does, the good work he has gotten ready for us to do, work we had better be doing.

> But don't take any of this for granted. It was only yesterday that you outsiders to God's ways had no idea of any of this, didn't know the first thing about the way God works, hadn't the faintest idea of Christ. (*Ephesians 2:7–11* MSG)

In your own words, how did you get here? How did you become a daughter of God? Spend some time reflecting before you begin writing. Allow yourself to go back and observe everything that has contributed to you becoming a royal daughter.

_____

_____

_____

_____

_____

What role did you play in saving yourself? Consider your response when God first appeared on your radar, entered your life, or when you realized He was a part of your life. Did you respond? Did you rebel? Why and how did matter?

_____

_____

_____

_____

What do you feel obligated to do to keep your place or status in the kingdom?

_____

_____

_____

_____

For all have sinned and fall short of the glory of God, and all are justified freely by his grace through the redemption that came by Christ Jesus.

—Romans 3:23–24

Why do you think it's easier to try to earn our place in the kingdom rather than just celebrate the grace that brought us here?

_____

_____

_____

_____

_____

How do you think God feels when you strive for your ideal self in light of the great grace He's lavished on you?

_____

_____

_____

But just as he who called you is holy, so be holy in all you do; for it is written, "Be holy, because I am holy."

—1 Peter 1:16

Now that we're here alone, with nobody watching but you and God, I have a really honest question for you: What are you trying to be the best at?

_____

_____

If you are struggling to find an answer, I have a follow-up question: Could you potentially be trying to be the best at not caring if you're the best? What does that look like? How is it keeping you from experiencing personal value, confidence, a spirit of gratitude for all you are?

_____

_____

_____

_____

How would your soul feel if you were to take a deep breath and perceive that you were off the hook, just for a day?

_____

_____

What would happen if you continued to miss the moment? What might you miss out on if you continually try to be the hero or if you continually discount yourself from having any potential part in God's rescue plan?

_____

_____

_____

What might happen if you *didn't* miss the moment? What might you see in the kingdom of God because you believed in His capacity, power, and presence in your life?

_____

_____

_____

DAY TWO:
HEAD

I don't want to just tell you to quit trying to hold it altogether, quit trying to be the best, if we can't trust that God's capacity truly will be enough. Let's engage our head and our minds, dig into God's Word and see if we can't find some biblical proof that we can quit striving, pretending, and let God be the hero.

First, let's do this:

Write an encouraging handful of lines that you would love to receive from a friend to make you feel capable, ready, prepared, worthy. Maybe something like, "You've got this! You were born for this!"

_____

_____

_____

_____

If anyone in the Word of God were ever in need of a pep talk, it was Moses on the mountain of Horeb, just before he'd answer the call to go to Pharaoh on behalf of his people.

Let's refresh ourselves a little with where we find Moses.

Read Exodus 3:1–10 and write any observations you have about what God is asking Moses to do.

_____

_____

_____

Now read Exodus 3:11. What is the singular question Moses has in response to the task God is giving him?

_____

Now read Exodus 3:12. What is God's response to Moses' question?

_____

_____

_____

Maybe many of us are craving an encouraging word, a handful of empowering statements not just from our friends but from God.

But ultimately, we don't find God telling Moses how great Moses is; we find God reminding Moses of who He is and that He'll be with him.

Let's look at a few other times in Scripture where God outlined a task for humans and what He told them to encourage them accept the call.

Read Genesis 46:2–4.

What is God asking Jacob to do?

_____

What reassurance does He give Jacob to complete the task?

_____

_____

Read Luke 1:26–35.

What is God asking Mary to do?

_____

_____

_____

What reassurance does He give Mary to obediently move forward?

_____

_____

_____

Read Matthew 28:16–20.

What is Jesus commissioning the disciples to do?

_____

_____

_____

What reassurance does He give them about how they'll accomplish the task?

_____

_____

_____

So here's my question: Do you know what God is asking *you* to do?

You have this whole video study, the entire *You Are the Girl for the Job* book to guide you, to sort through what God may be calling you to in this season of life. But if you had to say right now, in private, is there something He's put on your heart to accomplish, some area in which you need to obediently move forward, what would it be?

Write it here:

_____

_____

_____

_____

Now, instead of the pep talk you imagined in the beginning of today's work, how would you want to rewrite the encouraging words that will help you feel prepared using the passages of Scripture we've read today?

Hint: These words should have more to do with God's capacity, power, and presence than anything about you. If you need a little help, here are a few other verses of Scripture you can reference for help:

- Isaiah 41:10

- Ephesians 6:10

- 2 Thessalonians 3:3

Rewrite the encouraging words you need to hear here:

_____

_____

_____

_____

DAY THREE:
HANDS

GRATITUDE

Today, let's actively quit. Let's make movements and participate in actions that agree with the capacity, power, and presence of God.

First: There is one specific posture we can take to acknowledge the fact that the goodness and grace of God alone are responsible for anything that happens in our life. *Gratitude.*

Being grateful reminds us that He is the giver of all good gifts. Let's take some time to be grateful and remember that gratitude is not a passive practice. Gratitude is worshipful warfare, declaring that He is God and He is good and He has brought what we've needed.

What are you grateful for? List here and now everything you are grateful for.

_____

_____

_____

_____

_____

Now, spend a minute or two reflecting on your list. Notice the connection between what you are grateful for and God's capacity to meet your needs. Try to summarize your list into a word or phrase you can use to fill in the statement below:

Heavenly Father, I am so grateful for your _____.

QUITTING

We've talked a lot this week about quitting, but let's put some action toward this attitude. Here are the ground rules.

If you've committed to something and someone else is counting on you to complete it, it's important that you be a woman of your word. Girded by and compelled by grace, you get to walk through this process empowered by the Holy Spirit in a respectful and responsible way.

Are there any responsibilities that you are currently committed to for your *own glory*? Daily rhythms you are following that give personal, glorified satisfaction? If so, list them below. (*Examples: I get to work before everyone, I started a diet, I signed up to volunteer again even though I already serve somewhere else, I go overboard when planning my kids' birthday parties, I am the one who always brings coffee and goodies.*)

_____

_____

_____

_____

For the responsibilities or commitments that others are counting on you for, what would it look like to quit? Not abruptly, of course, but responsibly? Would there be drastic consequences/no consequences/temporary hurt/major inconvenience?

_____

_____

_____

_____

For the rhythms or commitments that people are *not* counting on your for, can you quit today? Can you acknowledge that any and all commitments that are self-glorifying keep us from glorifying God? Describe the ways in which quitting will free you up to glorify God.

_____

_____

_____

_____

Write a quick pledge and purpose statement of why you're quitting and sign your name to it with the date.

_____

_____

_____

_____

_____

Signature _____

Date _____

I'm proud of you!

EXPECTANCY

You might not always get what you want, but you always get what you expect. | Charles Spurgeon

Gratitude helps us quit and committing to quitting helps us release our world back to the capacity and power of God, but we can't end there.

We also get to put expectancy into our spiritual lives as well.

What are you expecting God to do in your life today?

_____

_____

_____

_____

_____

Who are you expecting Him to be?

_____

_____

_____

_____

_____

Search the following Bible passages for some of God's promises regarding His power and His presence.

- **Character of God:** Psalm 18:30; Isaiah 41:10; 2 Peter 3:9; 1 John 1:9; 1 John 4:8

- **Promises of God:** Exodus 14:14; Psalm 34:17; Isaiah 40:29, John 14:13–16; James 1:5

- **What we can expect:** Psalm 27:14; Psalm 37:4; Hosea 6:3; Romans 8:28; 1 Corinthians 10:13

Write truth-filled statements of expectation regarding His character and capacity in your life:

God's character is: _____

God promises me: _____

Because of who He is, I am expectant of: _____

God's character is: _____

God promises me: _____

Because of who He is, I am expectant of: _____

God's character is: _____

God promises me: _____

Because of who He is, I am expectant of: _____

COUNT THE FRUIT

> *I am the vine; you are the branches. If you remain in me and I in you, you will bear much fruit; apart from me you can do nothing.*
>
> —John 15:5

Before you gather with your group again, take a moment to count the fruit. Identify what God has grown in and through you this week:

God has accomplished _____ in me this week.

God has shown me _____ .

God has answered my question(s) of _____ .

God has reminded me of His capacity in this way this week:

_____

_____

_____

_____

God has shifted me, changed my mindset, altered my personal perspective in these ways:

_____

_____

_____

_____

_____

When we abide and remain in God's presence by praying, studying His Word, and even asking introspective questions, He grows us.

DAYS FOUR & FIVE
(OPTIONAL)

Read chapters 4–6 in the *You Are the Girl for the Job* book. **Reading through the book will enhance your experience of this study, but it is NOT required.**

WHO?

SCHEDULE

Review this week's schedule as a group before opening your time together.

BEFORE THE GROUP MEETING	Read the introduction and chapters 1–3 in *You Are the Girl for the Job* book.*
IN YOUR GROUP	• Welcome from Jess • Set the Temperature (prayer) • Personal Heart Check-In • Watch the video teaching for Session 2 and take notes • Complete Discussion Questions • Change the Language/Change the Culture • My Prayer + Your Prayer
AT HOME	• Personal Study Day 1 (engage your heart with God's love) • Personal Study Day 2 (fill your head with God's truth) • Personal Study Day 3 (agree with abundance)
PREP FOR NEXT GROUP MEETING	Count the fruit of what God's done. Read chapters 7–9 in the *You Are the Girl for the Job* book.*

Reading through the book will enhance your experience of this study, but it is NOT required.

GROUP STUDY

WELCOME NOTE FROM JESS (2 MINUTES)

Leader, *read the note from Jess aloud to the group.*

Alright gals, I hope you've quit.

During our last time together we committed to quitting the unhealthy motivations that keep us from experiencing His capacity. We quit trying to be our ideal selves and reminded our hearts that it's His grace that does the making and the saving. It's His grace that brings the power, so that's where we want to be.

I often get to meet with women who feel called by God to do something. They want to start a ministry, write a book, create a business, or they just feel excited about a new area of service that has been presented to them. Their excitement gets me excited. I love getting to function as a midwife of mission—getting pumped about what God is birthing in other women!

You can imagine with as many women as I talk to, I see a lot of failed attempts at projects or purposes that were seemingly given by God. I see a lot of things not pan out; or I see women thrilled at the start but never taking steps of obedience.

I've learned that I can almost always see one thread of similarity between the talks of excited planning and dreaming and the fruition of a God dream, or a calling. The women who talk to me about *who* they're going to serve and how their gifts will help them, I almost always see them take obedient steps. It's the women who tell me about the burden they have, the good they want for other people—that's the stuff that lasts.

Sadly, if someone just tells me they want to be something great or do something great for God, no matter how much I love them, I have to push them to think about their who—or else, there could be so much pain headed their way.

This wild and wonderful question will change our lives if we let it: Whose team am I on?

Everyone else asks: Who is on my team? But if we'll shift our focus and open our hands and widen our circles, I believe we'll find the power and purpose that keeps us going for as long as God wants us to—and keeps the eternal fruit of our mission coming long past our time.

This week we're going to talk about who our people are, and we're going to turn that question on its head—maybe in ways you may never have asked it. Let's dig in!

SET THE TEMPERATURE (2 MINUTES)

Pick someone to pray for the group before we do our personal heart check.

PERSONAL HEART CHECK (3 MINUTES)

Before we dig into this session's video, let's do a quick personal heart check. Take a minute or two to answer the following questions. You don't have to share these answers; this is just for you to pause and get honest with yourself and God.

A. On a scale of 1–10 1 (1 = very little, 10 = significantly), how much do you believe that God can change your life and change the world through you?

1   2   3   4   5   6   7   8   9   10

B. How does the idea of "tribe" make you feel? (Circle, underline, or highlight which option you resonate with most.)

GRATEFUL   EXCITED   SAD   LONELY   DOUBTFUL   CONFUSED

C. How willing are you to be surprised by God this week? (Circle, underline, or highlight how you feel this week.)

WON'T HAPPEN   THAT SOUNDS NICE   TEACH ME, CHANGE ME, SURPRISE ME

VIDEO TEACHING (21 MINUTES)

Watch the Session 2 video. Fill in the blanks throughout the teaching if you'd like:

- Jesus surrounded himself with those who would help him _____ _____

- Are you _____ _____ with anyone outside of where you are comfortable and safe?

- Moses: Who will _____ _____ be?

Who are your people?

Circle One:

People who provide safety and world comfort?

OR

The people who help you see the kingdom of heaven come to earth?

Father, help us see others how You do.

Take notes if you'd like:

Answer key: bring glory to God, being vulnerable, your people

GROUP DISCUSSION (30 MINUTES)

Leader, read each question aloud to the group. Take turns/volunteers for any Scripture reading.

1. Where do you fall on the scale of being lonely to totally feeling like you fit in? What do you use to measure where you fall (comparison to others, past experience, direct knowledge)? Discuss where our perception of where we fall in the social chasm comes from.

2. Why do you think the enemy tries to isolate women when it comes to community? Discuss what isolation feels like for the individual as well as what it makes you think about a person who is isolated. Are these ideas of yourself and others who are isolated valid or lies to keep the isolated person isolated?

3. What would an outward-facing, others-centered community look like to you? Discuss what it would or does feel like to be a part of this type of community. Does such a community seem utopic or possible? Why or why not?

4. **Look up and Read Acts 2:42–47 aloud.** This is a passage often held up as an incredible example for an impactful community. What do you feel most drawn to in the passage? What does this passage inspire you to bring to the table in your current group? Discuss any barriers you have met or perceive in the Acts 2 community. being a reality in your life.

CHANGE THE LANGUAGE, CHANGE THE CULTURE (10 MINUTES)

When we change the language, we change the culture. When we put different words in our mouths, words that agree with God's character and capacity, things begin to shift not only in our lives but also in our communities.

Read Proverbs 18:21 aloud together.

Select one person to read a statement on the left, and then have another person read the alternate statement on the right. Talk about the difference you hear and feel in each change in the language. Discuss how these simple shifts in our language can effect change in our immediate culture. Commit to using language with one another that agrees with God's Word.

INSTEAD OF:	TRY THIS:
I've always been left out. No one seems to want to spend time with me.	God has been with me in every season.
I'm not sure who my people are.	I can't wait to see who God has placed in my life on purpose.
Your vibe attracts your tribe.	God will unite our hearts with a similar passion for serving others.
You're my ride or die.	I love growing with you as we run on mission together.

Let's not take the bait of the enemy and use talk of community to complain or find fault in others. Rather, let's talk about what could be; let's talk about what He's growing in and through us. Let's go first and be the women who courageously let Him build abundant community through us and for us.

If our job is to use what we have for the good of others and the glory of God, we need core people in our lives with whom we can walk with and be encouraged by. But let's also widen the circle and practice being present to the people around us to whom God may be giving us opportunities to bless, encourage, enrich, and serve.

UP NEXT

Leader, *before dismissing remind the group of what comes next.*

- Count the fruit of what God's done and write it down or share with someone.

_____

_____

_____

_____

_____

- There are three days of personal study time to complete before we meet again.

- Read chapters 7–9 in *You Are the Girl for the Job* book if you are following along.

MY PRAYER + YOUR PRAYER (10 MINUTES)

Each week ask a volunteer to read the short prayer for the group, *and* each of you will also write a short prayer for yourself. Where are you asking God to meet you this week? What are you hoping will happen?

Father, I thank You for a moment to pause and ask who our people are. I'm also asking you for something wild right now—a shift in our current Christian culture. Make us women who are so wildly inclusive and excited about others. Give us eyes to see, ears to hear, hands that serve, and feet that itch to run and be about the good of others instead of ourselves. Meet us in our lonely places and bring partners, not so we can stay hidden together, but so that we can run forward in the light of your grace—on mission together. Amen.

Your turn:

_____

_____

_____

_____

_____

_____

PERSONAL
STUDY

DAY ONE:
HEART

CONFESS

By now you've read the recounting of my infamous spin class with David (from the introduction of *You Are the Girl for the Job*). Do you remember one of the things he said to our entire class: *You'll repeat what you don't repair.* In this first day of heart work regarding who your people are, I want to give you space to let God do some repairing in your heart. For sure, it may take more than one day, but let's get the process started. **First, is there anything regarding friend groups or community that you need to repent of? Confess it in writing here. Leave it here.**

Read Acts 3:19–21. Note what is on the other side of repentance for you:

_____

_____

_____

_____

_____

Here are a few prompts of attitude or activities that many of us have engaged in when it comes to community. If one comes to mind that I didn't list, don't let me stop you. Add to the list any behaviors or responses or attitudes that come to mind in reference to friend groups and/or community. Circle any you have engaged in this week. Underline any you have engaged in EVER.

GOSSIP	JUDGMENT	COMPARISON
ANGER	EXCLUSIVITY	MANIPULATION
DOUBT	SELFISHNESS	ASSUMPTIONS
DISCOUNTING	JEALOUSY	BACKSTABBING

_____

_____

_____

_____

Read **Romans 8:1** and write it here:

_____

_____

_____

_____

Be encouraged. God's grace is big enough to handle your sin. To complete this work of confession, is there anyone you need to apologize to or ask forgiveness from? If so, share their name below and covenant with yourself to do that soon.

_____

_____

_____

HEALING

Most of us will find that we've been complicit in the pain of others, and we're also in need of healing ourselves. We've been hurt and we can never guarantee that the other humans involved will be at the same point of repentance that we are.

Let me ask a few questions to get to the heart of healing, or at the very least, the *start* of healing. **How have you been hurt in the past when it comes to community? Briefly describe the situation(s).**

_____

_____

_____

In this or those situations, who was the enemy?

_____

_____

_____

_____

_____

Read John 10:10 and answer the question again. Who was the enemy?

_____

_____

_____

_____

_____

I find that when it comes to receiving healing from past pain, it really helps me to remember who the enemy is. The enemy is not the human who hurt me; that person is flesh and blood like me, able to hurt and able to help, but often getting sidetracked by the schemes of the enemy. The real enemy of your soul is Satan. But thankfully, he's not the final word in any of our lives. We look at the life of Joseph a few times in *You Are the Girl for the Job*, but I want you to look briefly at something powerful and poignant that Joseph said in Genesis 50.

_____

_____

_____

_____

_____

Read Genesis 50:20.

Who was the enemy in Joseph's life?

_____

How did Joseph use forgiveness and hope to defeat that enemy?

_____

_____

_____

_____

REDEMPTION

The most beautiful thing about pain or hardship that you've endured or pain or hardship that you've caused is that you can learn from it, grow, and experience redemption. Thank you, Jesus, for that!

_____

_____

_____

_____

Write down some ways you can see that God has used the pain you've experienced as it pertains to community and turned it into something beautiful?

_____

_____

_____

Write down some of the ways you'd love to see Him use the pain you've caused as it pertains to community?

_____

_____

_____

Turn those thoughts into a prayer of gratitude and a prayer for redemption. You are the girl for the job.

DAY TWO:
HEAD

A passage of Scripture that has always massively encouraged me when it comes to community is Luke 14. Head there with me now and see what you can learn from it.

Read all of Luke 14:1–24.

Jesus does a lot of teaching in this short passage. Notice who He is teaching at different points.

If you could summarize what He's trying to teach the Pharisees in verses 1–6, what do you think He's trying to show them? Put it in your own words.

_____

_____

For me, what I hear from Jesus in this particular short passage is: *People over processes.* The Sabbath is a beautiful rhythm given by God to help us deepen our experience with Him. But the people we encounter in the midst of any process have to matter more than the process itself.

Is there a rhythm or a process that is so important to you, you often find yourself neglecting the people God has put in your path? *Examples: Prioritizing alone time and not caring for family, insisting on getting your house clean and missing out on time in community.*

When you read verses 7–11, as Jesus is teaching the guests, what's the main message you hear? Put it in your own words.

_____

_____

I think about times when I'm a guest or when I wish I had been invited. The invitation feels like the honor, and I often forget that the real honor of my life is being a friend of Jesus. Sometimes I forget to think through how I can honor others, see others, and point them to God when I'm invited.

Recount a place you were honored to be invited or wish you would be invited:

_____

Briefly describe how you could honor or serve others in that place:

_____

_____

Next read verses 12–14, a teaching for the hosts of the party. Summarize the message of Jesus here:

_____

_____

It's interesting to me that we often have to think through this issue of honor and humility and *who matters* not only as guests, but also as hosts.

Is there a space that is yours to shepherd? An event you're hosting at your home, in your neighborhood, or even at your office? Describe an opportunity God has given you to shepherd here:

_____

_____

Describe ways you could consider those who are often not considered:

_____

_____

Finally, read verses 15–24. What do you notice in this portion of the passage? What stands out to you?

_____

_____

This parable is about the kingdom and those who will be invited and those who can't be bothered to come. But I think it's such a great moment for you to pause as you're spending time determining *who* God has called you to serve.

Here's the one last question from this passage: What would it look like in your life to "go out to the roads and country lanes and compel them to come in"? Describe what would change in your daily routine, your responses to situations and circumstances you encounter, how you approach others, and how you imagine you might feel.

_____

_____

_____

What do you think would happen if a generation of women cared less about who doesn't accept or approve of them and moved more toward loving and serving those who are unloved by others? Dream and be realistic here. Don't underestimate the power of envisioned change that leads to actual change.

_____

_____

_____

DAY THREE:
HANDS

Today take all your head and heart knowledge and put some strategy and action around what you've learned.

IDENTIFY

Who is already listening to you? *List the people you encounter every day who you may often forget you have impact on.*

_____

_____

Who do you feel called to serve, even if you haven't acted on it yet? *Is it a people group, a neighbor? List their names here.*

_____

_____

Take a moment and write some prayers for these specific people. Ask God to give you His eyes and ears to see and hear what they're dealing with. Ask Him to give you vision for how to serve them. Ask Him to increase your capacity and your love. Ask Him to provide you with time to be the hands and feet of Jesus to His creation.

ENCOURAGE

Therefore encourage one another and build one another up, just as you are doing.

—1 Thessalonians 5:11

When we've identified a few people that we know we're called to love, sometimes we can feel stuck about how to serve or love them. In our next session, we're going to explore what God has placed in our hands for the good of others and the glory of God, but let's start with encouragement.

How can you specifically encourage the people God has put on your heart? List 1–3 ways.

1. _____

2. _____

3. _____

Run to God's Word when you're stuck. If you need specific words to encourage others and you don't feel like you have them, here are a few that I highly suggest. Look up and read each of these verses, then text them to a friend, email them, or write a handwritten card. God's Word does not fail! It is meant to be shared and used for building one another up!

Psalm 31:24   Luke 1:37   Colossians 1:11
Romans 15:13   Psalm 16:11

COUNT THE FRUIT

> *I am the vine; you are the branches. If you remain in me and I in you, you will bear much fruit; apart from me you can do nothing.*
>
> —John 15:5

Before you gather with your group again, take a moment to count the fruit. Here's what I mean by that: identify what God has grown in and through you this week.

God has accomplished _____ in me this week.

God has shown me _____.

God has answered my question(s) of _____.

God has reminded me of His capacity in this way this week:

_____

_____

_____

_____

God has shifted me, changed my mindset, altered my personal perspective in these ways:

_____

_____

_____

_____

> When we abide and remain in God's presence by praying, studying His Word, and even asking introspective questions, He grows us.

DAYS FOUR & FIVE
(OPTIONAL)

Read chapters 7–9 in the *You Are the Girl for the Job* book. **Reading through the book will enhance your experience of this study, but it is NOT required.**

WHAT?

SCHEDULE

Review this week's schedule as a group before opening your time together.

BEFORE THE GROUP MEETING	Read Chapters 7–9 in *You Are the Girl for the Job* book.
IN YOUR GROUP	<ul><li>Welcome from Jess</li><li>Set the Temperature (prayer)</li><li>Personal Heart Check-In</li><li>Watch the video teaching for Session 3 and take notes</li><li>Complete Discussion Questions</li><li>Change the Language/Change the Culture</li><li>My Prayer + Your Prayer</li></ul>
AT HOME	<ul><li>Personal Study Day 1 (engage your heart with God's love)</li><li>Personal Study Day 2 (fill your head with God's truth)</li><li>Personal Study Day 3 (agree with abundance)</li></ul>
PREP FOR NEXT GROUP MEETING	Count the fruit of what God's done. Read chapters 10–12 in the *You Are the Girl for the Job* book.*

Reading through the book will enhance your experience of this study, but it is NOT required.

GROUP STUDY

WELCOME NOTE FROM JESS (2 MINUTES)

Leader, read note from Jess aloud to the group

Friends! We've quit striving and trying to be the hero. We've asked God *who* He's given us to love. And now it's time that we look down at our hands, our lives, our stories—and figure out *what* He's given us to love others.

We may go somewhere this week that you don't expect. What we look at as it pertains to spiritual gifts and strengths may surprise you. Stay with me and stay expectant. Here's one of my favorite verses to kick us off:

The boundary lines have fallen for me in pleasant places; surely I have a delightful inheritance.

—Psalm 16:6

I believe He has drawn beautiful boundary lines when it comes to you and the gifts you've been given to change the world. Do you believe it?

SET THE TEMPERATURE (2 MINUTES)

Pick someone to pray for the group before we do our personal heart check.

Personal Heart Check (3 minutes)

Before we dig into this session's video, let's do a quick personal heart check. Take a minute or two to answer the following questions. You don't have to share these answers; this is just for you to pause and get honest with yourself and God.

A. On a scale of 1–10 (1 = very little, 10 = significantly), how much do you believe that God can change your life and change the world through you?

1   2   3   4   5   6   7   8   9   10

B. When you think of the gifts God has given you, how do you feel? (Circle, underline, or highlight which option you resonate with most.)

THANKFUL   EXCITED   CONFUSED   DISAPPOINTED   FEARFUL   GRATEFUL

C. How willing are you to be surprised by God this week? (Circle, underline, or highlight how you feel this week.)

WON'T HAPPEN   THAT SOUNDS NICE   TEACH ME, CHANGE ME, SURPRISE ME

VIDEO TEACHING (21 MINUTES)

Watch the Session 3 video. Fill in the blanks throughout the teaching if you'd like:

● Before we consider our strengths, let's consider our _____.

● Curious ego = the _____ of me.

● Rabboni = respectful; intimate; teacher & master with _____ implication of relationship.

- Jesus chose a _____ to be the first to relay the message he had risen.

- Mary took Jesus at _____ _____ and wanted other to see.

We're the kind of women God uses because we're open and eager to have His healing meet our brokenness.

Take notes if you'd like:

Answer key: weaknesses, master, personal, woman, His word

GROUP DISCUSSION (30 MINUTES)

Leader, read each question aloud to the group. Take turns/volunteers for any Scripture reading.

1. Was anyone surprised about Mary's testimony? Why?

2. Does anything frighten you about starting with weaknesses when we think about strengths? Explain.

3. Have you ever experienced the kind of grace that spurs you on to tell other people about Jesus? Or, have you ever heard someone else tell you about a grace experience that he/she could not keep quiet about? Share an example.

4. **Look up and read 2 Corinthians 12:9 aloud.** Taking turns, translate this verse, inserting each your own personal weaknesses and declaring the truth of how God will help you overcome them. *Example: I will thank God and admit my struggles with insecurity. I believe that when I submit this weakness to Him— God's power will be put on display and He'll use me even more than I imagined.*

CHANGE THE LANGUAGE, CHANGE THE CULTURE (20 MINUTES)

Friends, I'm a big believer in this idea: when we change the language, we change the culture. Here's what I mean: when we put different words in our mouths, words that agree with God's character and capacity, things begin to shift not only in our lives but also in our communities.

Read Proverbs 18:21 aloud together.

Select one person to read a statement on the left, and then have another person read the alternate statement on the right. Talk about the difference you hear and feel in each change of the language. Discuss how these simple shifts in our language can effect change in our immediate culture. Commit to using language with one another that agrees with God's Word.

INSTEAD OF:	TRY THIS:
I'm a mess.	God meets me in my weaknesses.
If people knew what I struggled with, they'd reject me.	God knew what I'd struggle with, and He still called me into His family and into His service.
I don't have any strengths.	My Father is a good giver. I can't wait to see what kind of strengths He has and will give me.
That person is too far gone.	That child of God is in the right place to be met by God and used by Him too.

READ THIS ALOUD IN UNISON.

When we've given up on the idea of fame and appreciation for our own sakes, when we've truly considered the good in those around us, after we push through all our fears about being obedient and pick up the tools placed inside us by a good Father, abundance comes. Joy comes. Freedom comes. And we might just *savor* utilizing our strengths.

UP NEXT

Leader, *before dismissing remind the group of what comes next.*

● Count the fruit of what God's done and write it down or share with someone.

_____

_____

_____

_____

● There are three days of personal study time to complete before we meet again.

● Read chapters 10–12 in *You Are the Girl for the Job* book if you are following along.

MY PRAYER + YOUR PRAYER (10 MINUTES)

Each week I'll write a short prayer for you, and you to also write a short prayer for yourself. What are you asking God for this week? What are you hoping will happen?

> *Father, I praise You for our weaknesses! You've allowed them on purpose for some reason, and honestly we're grateful. We don't want a powerless ministry, so we're ready to use what we've been given with intention and expectation. You didn't stop there though; You also gave us some strengths, some gifts, some tools to be used in positive and life-giving ways. Will You help us to move forward with humility and hope, seeing what we've been given and not being scared of what may happen when we step into our strengths? Thank you so much for the wisdom and help You bring. In Jesus' name, amen.*

Your turn:

_____

_____

_____

_____

_____

_____

_____

PERSONAL STUDY

DAY ONE:
HEART

THOUGHTS FROM JESS

I won't lie to you! This is where everything shifts for me, friend.

Show me a woman who has a vibrant and open relationship with God, her Father, who sees Him as generous and kind. Show me a woman who believes that her weaknesses have been allowed on purpose for her good and their glory. Show me a woman who steps into her strengths with humility and hope, ready to be used by God.

This is a woman who is living in abundance. I also believe that many of us have unintentionally believed some funky stuff in our hearts and our minds about using what we have and that it's time to untangle those lies. The enemy of our souls would so love for us to believe that our weaknesses prohibit us from being used by God or that our strengths are better hidden and undiscovered.

So, draw near to the heart of God with belief and hope, and get some wisdom from the right source. Amen? Amen.

SELF-EXAMINATION

In the first day of this session's personal study, I want you to do a quick heart check regarding your perception of God's character and His heart toward you. What causes many women to hide their weaknesses and doubt the existence of their strengths is a distorted perception of their heavenly Father.

Do you believe that God holds out on you? Why? In what ways?

_____

_____

_____

_____

Do you believe that God is generous to some and not to others? Why? How?

_____

_____

_____

_____

Do you believe that you're usable by God just as you are today? Why or why not? How might you be usable?

_____

_____

_____

_____

Do you believe that He wants good for you and that He wants to bring good from your life? Why or why not?

_____

_____

_____

_____

_____

I find that most of us will find evidence to support what we want to believe or what is easy to believe. And so, if we try, we can find evidence to support the lies that set themselves up against the knowledge of God.

Commit to being a woman who looks for evidence to support TRUTH. Look up the following passages and then count the ways you've seen this to be true in your life. Write them out here.

2 Corinthians 9:8–11

_____

_____

I've seen this to be true in my life:

_____

_____

_____

_____

Philippians 4:19

_____

_____

I've seen this to be true in my life:

_____

_____

_____

_____

Ephesians 1:3

_____

_____

I've seen this to be true in my life:

_____

_____

_____

_____

The question of whether or not God will give you what we need, and more than that, whether or not He'll generously provide power and strength for you to do His will, can either draw you nearer to Him or push you further away.

Please allow the truth and power of His person compel you closer, increase your intimacy, and bind you nearer to the heart of your good and generous Father.

DAY TWO:
HEAD

Today, let's put a bit of head knowledge behind the answer to this question: where did our gifts come from? Head to 2 Timothy for some answers.

Read 2 Timothy 1:1–7.

Who is Paul writing to?

_____

_____

_____

How would you summarize this part of his message?

_____

_____

_____

I want to focus mostly on **2 Timothy 1:6** . Please write the verse in the space below to solidify it in your heart.

_____

_____

_____

_____

When I'm really wanting to unpack a passage, my favorite thing to do is look up the Greek or Hebrew the original passage was written in. That always tends to unlock a little more meaning for me. Let's do that here.

There are two words/phrases I want to focus on.

GIFT

Greek word: χάρισμα or charisma – def. translation in this verse is *a free gift of grace*.

> Now consider another passage where this verse is used. Look up and write out **Romans 6:23** in the space below, underlining "gift" in the verse:
>
> _____
>
> _____
>
> _____
>
> _____

Okay! We get this grace, we know this grace! It's God coming toward us with something we don't deserve. It's salvation, eternal life, abundance! We know this grace!

Let's look at one other word in the passage:

FAN INTO FLAME

Greek word: ἀναζωπυρέω, or anazópureó – def. translation *"fan into flame"*

Interestingly, this word is used only here in the entire New Testament, so we need to dig a little further if we want to see it in a stronger sense.

It's a compound of two root words: zóon and pur, with the preposition ana kicking the whole thing off. Here are what each of those words mean individually:

- **ana:** def. translation *upward*

- **zóon:** def. translation *living creature*

- **pur:** def. translation *eternal or holy fire*

Whoosh, when you smoosh all those words together, it makes a beautiful word picture, right? Write it out altogether here:

_____

_____

_____

Look with me at one other place that the word pur is found in the New Testament. Read **Matthew 3:11** and get ready to dig around a little. Write the verse below:

_____

_____

_____

_____

Who is speaking in this verse?

_____

_____

_____

And who is John the Baptist speaking about?

_____

_____

_____

And what does this passage say that Jesus will baptize us with?

_____

_____

_____

That's right—the Holy Spirit and *fire.*

When we hold all these passages together, consider the important questions that follow:

Where do our gifts come from?

_____

_____

_____

What did we do to deserve them?

_____

_____

_____

Are they alive or dead?

_____

_____

_____

Who gave the gift?

_____

_____

_____

If the gifts we've been given are from God, made alive by the power of His Holy Spirit and the resurrection power that raised Him from the dead, then maybe we should use them.

If the gifts we've been given are an expression of His grace, the unmerited favor of God that we don't deserve and cannot earn, then maybe we should use them.

If the gifts need to be stoked and prodded and spurred on to reach their full burning potential, then maybe this is all worth talking about, learning about, and praying through. Amen? Amen.

DAY THREE:
HANDS

Get ready to put into practice what you've received in your heart and in your mind!

PRAY WITH A PARTNER

Read Ecclesiastes 4:9–12.

Why is it better to have a partner?

_____

_____

_____

The first thing I'm going to encourage you to do this week is ask someone to pray with you! Here are a few things you can ask a partner to pray with you about:

- Ask a friend to pray for you as you seek to find out what your gifts are.

- Ask a friend to pray against fear as you step into them.

- Ask a friend to pray for belief in God's power and capacity in your life.

And then—PRAY FOR THEM.

Who will you ask to partner in prayer with you this week?

_____

SAY YES TO A PREVIOUS NO

As we seek to be obedient in letting God use both our weaknesses and our strengths, identify if there's something you've said no to in the past that you need to say yes to in the future.

In what ways have your weaknesseses ever held you back?

_____

_____

What does God's Word say about your own weaknesses? And His power?

_____

_____

In what ways have you said no to something because you believe your strength may fail? Or because you might not have what it takes?

_____

_____

What does God's Word say about your strength? And who has what it takes?

_____

What have you said no to in the past that you need to say yes to moving forward?

_____

_____

LEARN MORE

Take some time this week to dig into learning more about your particular God-given gifts. Here are a few resources I can't suggest enough.

- The Five-Fold Gifting Test

- The Enneagram Institute

- Strength Finders Test

COUNT THE FRUIT

I am the vine; you are the branches. If you remain in me and I in you, you will bear much fruit; apart from me you can do nothing.

—John 15:5

Before you gather with your group again, take a moment to count the fruit. Here's what I mean by that: identify what God has grown in and through you this week.

God has accomplished _____ in me this week.

God has shown me _____.

God has answered my question(s) of _____.

God has reminded me of His capacity in this way this week:

_____

_____

_____

_____

God has shifted me, changed my mindset, altered my personal perspective in these ways:

_____

_____

_____

_____

When we abide and remain in God's presence by praying, studying His Word, and even asking introspective questions, He grows us.

DAYS FOUR & FIVE
(OPTIONAL)

Read chapters 10–12 in the *You Are the Girl for the Job* book. **Reading through the book will enhance your experience of this study, but it is NOT required.**

FACE THE FEAR

SCHEDULE

Review this week's schedule as a group before opening your time together.

BEFORE THE GROUP MEETING

Read chapters 10–12 in the *You Are the Girl for the Job* book.*

IN YOUR GROUP

- Welcome from Jess
- Set the Temperature (prayer)
- Personal Heart Check-In
- Watch the video teaching for Session 4 and take notes
- Complete Discussion Questions
- Change the Language/Change the Culture
- My Prayer + Your Prayer

AT HOME

- Personal Study Day 1 (engage your heart with God's love)
- Personal Study Day 2 (fill your head with God's truth)
- Personal Study Day 3 (agree with abundance)

PREP FOR NEXT GROUP MEETING

Count the fruit of what God's done. Read chapters 13–15 in the *You Are the Girl for the Job* book.*

Reading through the book will enhance your experience of this study, but it is NOT required.

GROUP STUDY

WELCOME NOTE FROM JESS (2 MINUTES)

Leader, *read the note from Jess aloud to the group.*

Oh ladies. Are we going to have some fun this week or what?

We're not slaves to fear, we're not children of fear! And it's time to do some serious battle against what holds us back from obedience.

Take courage, this is going to be great.

SET THE TEMPERATURE (2 MINUTES)

Pick someone to pray for the group before we do our personal heart check.

PERSONAL HEART CHECK (3 MINUTES)

Before we dig into this session's video, let's do a quick personal heart check. Take a minute or two to answer the following questions. You don't have to share these answers; this is just for you to pause and get honest with yourself and God.

A. On a scale of 1–10 (1 = very little, 10 = significantly), how much do you believe that God can change your life and change the world through you?

1   2   3   4   5   6   7   8   9   10

B. How would you describe your relationship with fear? (Circle, underline, or highlight which option you resonate with most.)

WE'RE CLOSE   I HATE FEAR BUT STRUGGLE   I'M NOT SCARED
                 WITH IT SOMETIMES   OF ANYTHING!

C. How willing are you to be surprised by God this week? (Circle, underline, or highlight how you feel this week.)

WON'T HAPPEN   THAT SOUNDS NICE   TEACH ME, CHANGE ME,
                                        SURPRISE ME

VIDEO TEACHING (19:30 MINUTES)

Watch Video Session 4. Fill in the blanks throughout the teaching if you like.

- The 4 Big Fears: failure, qualification, loss of comfort, approval

- Fear of Failure: _____ will see me fail. _____ will see me fail.

- _____ _____ of fear of failure. You are _____ _____ fail.

- God's qualification processes are _____ _____ humans.

- God will _____ _____ everything you need.

- Our human inadequacies _____ _____.

Fear will no longer hold us back from obedience or from the abundance that He's purchased for us!

Take notes if you'd like:

Answer key: people/God, let go/going to, not like, give you, don't disqualify

GROUP DISCUSSION (30 MINUTES)

Leader, *read each question aloud to the group. Take turns/volunteers for any Scripture reading.*

1. What are some silly, irrational things you're scared of?

2. Describe a time you have been truly terrified of something and it's happened? What was true of God when that occurred?

3. What will you potentially miss out on if you continue to listen to fear?

4. **Look up and Read 2 Corinthians 10:5 aloud.** Discuss what it looks like to be obedient in the face of fear.

CHANGE THE LANGUAGE, CHANGE THE CULTURE (20 MINUTES)

When we change the language, we change the culture. When we put different words in our mouths, words that agree with God's character and capacity, things begin to shift not only in our lives but also in our communities.

Read Proverbs 18:21 aloud together.

Select one person to read a statement on the left, and then have another person read the alternate statement on the right. Talk about the difference you hear and feel in each change of the language. Discuss how these simple shifts in our language can effect change in our immediate culture. Commit to using language with one another that agrees with God's Word.

INSTEAD OF:	TRY THIS:
I'm scared of everything!	I wasn't given a spirit of fear. I forget that sometimes, but I know who God made me to be.

INSTEAD OF:	TRY THIS:
I'm a people pleaser.	I'm here for God's glory and I already have His approval.
I could never do something brave like that.	God is increasing my faith in His capacity every day.
I'm scared to do it wrong!	I'm held by God's grace!

Let's ask God to help us watch all our language as it pertains to our strengths and our weaknesses. Is what we're saying biblical and true of His character? Are we speaking words that leave room for His redemption, His power, and His promises to take root?

READ THIS ALOUD IN UNISON.

Let's be women of love, not limited by what *might* come our way. Let's be women defined by action and activated faith, trusting God and His Word above how things look, how we feel, or what we fear. We are the girls for the job. We are the ones placed right where we need to be, on purpose, to live for His glory and to resist the scary things. You were made to worship through fear. We were made to see Him and His hand as bigger than anything headed our way.

UP NEXT

Leader, *before dismissing remind the group of what comes next .*

- Count the fruit of what God's done and write it down or share with someone.

_____

_____

_____

_____

_____

- There are three days of personal study time to complete before we meet again.

- Read chapters 15–16 in the *You Are the Girl for the Job* book if you are following along.

MY PRAYER + YOUR PRAYER (10 MINUTES)

Each week ask a volunteer to read the short prayer for the group, *and* you will also write a short prayer for yourself. Where are you asking God to meet you this week? What are you hoping will happen?

Father, give us the power to press past the fear and fall into wild faith. Give us such a holy and humbled view of You that we can't help but obediently move forward. Help us to treat fear like the liar and the bully that it is. Help us to remember that we're the girls for the job because You've placed us here on purpose.

Your turn:

_____

_____

_____

_____

_____

_____

_____

PERSONAL STUDY

DAY ONE:
HEART

The heart work I find we often have to with fear and where we have to start is acknowledging it.

You might have read my story in chapter 10 of *You Are the Girl for the Job*, the moment where I boldly declared, "I'm not scared of anything!" only to realize I was actually just scared of everything. Let me ask you a few questions to get honest with yourself and with God.

What do you already know you're scared of?

_____

What are you anxious about?

_____

What do you worry about?

_____

What are you cautious about?

_____

In what ways might your fear come across as strength or toughness?

_____

_____

_____

Women who know they're scared can start by combatting their fear in healthy and powerful ways. It's women who don't know just how scared they are, or who believe their fear to be God-given and approved, that often have a tougher time combatting this spiritual stronghold.

So one of the most important questions I want to ask you this week in regards to your fear is this: are you seeing things the way God sees them or are you assuming that God sees things the way you do?

Read **Isaiah 55:8–9** and write it below:

_____

_____

_____

_____

Now, rewrite the passage in your own words. Frame it so you that your words are personal and reflective of your current circumstance or life situation.

_____

_____

_____

So now, as you've taken God's Word into your own personal context, grab a few of the thoughts you wrote above and do some heart examining.

What's the fear or thought that has set itself up against what you know to be true of God?

_____

_____

Describe where or when you learned that idea or thought. What influenced your fearful perspective?

_____

_____

_____

What is the truth of God that combats or fights that fear? Hint: use God's Word!

_____

_____

What do you think will happen if you continue to listen to the fear? Describe what you might miss out on:

_____

_____

Describe what will happen if you don't listen to the fear:

_____

_____

DAY TWO:
HEAD

If in Day One of the personal study, we took a deep dive into your own heart and mind to examine where your fears might have come from and what might happen if you continue to harbor them. Today, let's study some truths that will help you develop NEW ideas and thoughts to fight the enemy.

Read **Romans 12:1-2** and paraphrase it in your own words below.

_____

_____

_____

_____

Scientists tell us that many fears are learned from experience. Our bodies sense danger, we become physically stimulated, and we use that adrenaline to process whatever feels like a threat. The problem is that once our brains learn that specific pathway of getting through a potential threat, they will continually respond that way—until we experience a new successful path.

This is an area where Scripture backs up the science, and science helps us understand how to live out Scripture well.

The patterns of this world are fear, death, and defeat, but our minds have the capacity to be renewed by the knowledge and practice of faith, victory, and worship.

Let's soak up what God's Word has to say about those three attributes that we have access to.

FAITH

Read Hebrews 11:1 and 2 Corinthians 5:7.

What does faith not come through?

_____

Write in your own words the correlation between what you've seen and what you fear.

_____

_____

_____

Read Romans 10:17.

Where can we count on faith to come from?

_____

If you want to form new pathways in your brain, new responses to any perceived threat or danger with faith, where should you turn to have your belief in God bolstered? Why is this important?

_____

_____

VICTORY

Read 1 Corinthians 15:57–58.

Where and when did victory come in our lives?

_____

Read Romans 8:31–39.

Here's one translation of Romans 8:37 that specifically speaks to my heart, found in the New Living Translation.

> *No, despite all these things, overwhelming victory is ours through Christ, who loved us.*
>
> —Romans 8:37 NLT

What kind of victory is ours?

_____

What can take that kind of victory away?

_____

How did we come to access it?

_____

Describe how your perspective would change if you believed with your whole heart and your whole mind that death was really not a threat anymore?

_____

_____

_____

_____

_____

_____

WORSHIP

If faith fights fear and victory reminds us that death is not a credible threat, then worship helps us fight the defeat that creeps in—causing us to feel afraid or busted. Worship creates new neurological pathways in our brain, helping us experiencing new reactions to potential dangers.

Tomorrow we'll talk about how to actively engage worship to fight fear.

DAY THREE:
HANDS

One of my most paralyzing fears of the recent past is flying. A few years ago, I had a really horrific flight with incredibly bad turbulence and since then I've been so scared whenever I fly. I was talking to my counselor about said fear and she told me:

> One time you were flying and had a bad experience, and your brain learned that fear got you on the ground safe. So you need to teach your brain that worship also leaves you safe.

> Ever since then, I've spent my flights not just trying NOT to be scared, but actively worshiping and teaching my brain new things, being renewed by the transformation of my mind, not continually conforming to the patterns I once learned.

So, to truly fight fear, we have to worship. *Let's go!*

SING A SONG

Read Psalm 100:1–5.

Make a short list of how you can fill your day with worshipful singing.

_____

_____

GO SCARED

Read Joshua 1:9.

My favorite thing about courage is that you don't have to wait till you're not scared to be courageous. Rather, you get to go forward in something you're afraid of—believing that God is with you. Write out 2–3 things you can do today, even while you're afraid. This is worship!

_____

_____

_____

Read Psalm 95:2–3.

We can fight fear with thanksgiving and gratitude, thanking God for how He's rescued us in the past, how He's helped us in the past, how He's been exactly what we've needed in terrifying situations. Recall His good deeds and thank Him. Make a short list here:

_____

_____

_____

You get to worship as a response to the fear that sets itself up between you and the knowledge that God is good and that He loves you. Fight with worship TODAY.

COUNT THE FRUIT

I am the vine; you are the branches. If you remain in me and I in you, you will bear much fruit; apart from me you can do nothing.

—John 15:5

Before you gather with your group again, take a moment to count the fruit. Here's what I mean by that: identify what God has grown in and through you this week.

God has accomplished _____ in me this week.

God has shown me _____.

God has answered my question(s) of _____.

God has reminded me of His capacity in this way this week:

_____

_____

_____

_____

God has shifted me, changed my mindset, altered my personal perspective in these ways:

_____

_____

_____

_____

> When we abide and remain in God's presence by praying, studying His Word, and even asking introspective questions, He grows us.

DAYS FOUR & FIVE
(OPTIONAL)

Read chapters 13–15 in the *You Are the Girl for the Job* book. **Reading through the book will enhance your experience of this study, but it is NOT required.**

5

CATCH THE VISION

SCHEDULE

Review this week's schedule as a group before opening your time together.

BEFORE THE GROUP MEETING	Read chapters 11–13 in the *You Are the Girl for the Job* book.*
IN YOUR GROUP	• Welcome from Jess • Set the Temperature (prayer) • Personal Heart Check-In • Watch the video teaching for Session 5 and take notes • Complete Discussion Questions • Change the Language/Change the Culture • My Prayer + Your Prayer
AT HOME	• Personal Study Day 1 (engage your heart with God's love) • Personal Study Day 2 (fill your head with God's truth) • Personal Study Day 3 (agree with abundance)
PREP FOR NEXT GROUP MEETING	Count the fruit of what God's done. Read chapters 14–16 in the *You Are the Girl for the Job* book.*

*Reading through the book will enhance your experience of this study, but it is NOT required.

GROUP STUDY

WELCOME NOTE FROM JESS

Leader, *read note from Jess aloud to the group.*

Welcome to what may be my favorite session in any Bible study I've ever gotten to be a part of. For the record, I fully consider myself a part of your group—I just wish I were there in the flesh!

I pray two things often when I'm teaching or leading at my church:

- I pray that the Holy Spirit would be a better communicator than I am.

- I pray that the Holy Spirit would be gentle and complete when communicating.

I love being a part of your group. I love getting to study with you. I love growing together in God's grace and the belief that He has called us the girls for the job. But as much as I love communicating with you, I know that God has more wisdom, more encouragement, and more life to speak over you than I could in one thousand Bible studies.

And that's where we find ourselves in this session—poised and ready to hear from God directly.

So, let me start by sharing one more phrase that I use a lot when I'm teaching:

"Hi, I'm Jess. I believe that when we talk to God, He hears us. And more than that, I believe He communicates back to us. So, let's catch a vision from Him that will keep us going, point us where He wants us to head, and empower us more than human words ever could."

Let's go!

SET THE TEMPERATURE (2 MINUTES)

Pick someone to open the group in prayer before we do our personal heart check.

Personal Heart Check (3 minutes)

Before we dig into this session's video, let's do a quick personal heart check. Take a minute or two to answer the following questions. You don't have to share these answers; this is just for you to pause and get honest with yourself and God.

A. On a scale of 1–10 (1 = very little, 10 = significantly), how much do you believe that God hears you?

1   2   3   4   5   6   7   8   9   10

B. When you think of Him sharing insight and wisdom with you, how do you feel? (Circle, underline, or highlight which option you resonate with most.)

DOUBTFUL   THANKFUL   CONFUSED   EXCITED   AMBIVALENT

C. How willing are you to be surprised by God this week? (Circle, underline, or highlight how you feel this week.)

WON'T HAPPEN   THAT SOUNDS NICE   TEACH ME, CHANGE ME, SURPRISE ME

VIDEO TEACHING (17 MINUTES)

Watch Video Session 5 and fill in the blanks throughout the teaching if you like.

● God. He's the _____. He's the _____.

● Joseph was a man of great patience because he _____ _____.

● God is not _____ _____ on any of his daughters.

● Expect him. Your capacity is _____ the variable.

The experiences you have with God do not ride on your adequacy, but on your willingness to hear Him.

Take notes if you'd like:

GROUP DISCUSSION (30 MINUTES)

Leader, read each question aloud to the group. Take turns/volunteers for any Scripture reading.

1. Do you ever struggle to believe that God wants to give you vision or insight? Why? What gets in your way?

2. How have you heard from God in the past? How did you know it was God? Did you confirm or affirm what you heard in any way? What gave you the confidence to believe what you heard?

3. Is there a time when God gave you insight or vision into a hard or amazing season and it really helped you?

4. How does it make you feel that the vision may not be one of the "stage"? What if the vision and insight God gives you is strength and joy for the shadows? How does that change your response to the vision or your perception of it?

CHANGE THE LANGUAGE, CHANGE THE CULTURE (20 MINUTES)

When we change the language, we change the culture. When we put different words in our mouths, words that agree with God's character and capacity, things begin to shift not only in our lives but also in our communities.

Read Proverbs 18:21 aloud together.

Select one person to read a statement on the left, and then have another person read the alternate statement on the right. Talk about the difference you hear and feel in each change of the language. Discuss how these simple shifts in our language can effect change in our immediate culture. Commit to using language with one another that agrees with God's Word.

INSTEAD OF:	TRY THIS:
I don't hear from God like that.	God does not hold back from me.
I don't know how to hear from God.	I'm learning to discern the voice of God.
I'm not sure where to go next.	I can't wait for God to give me insight about what's next.
I'm going to do something big for God.	God has done something big for me.

READ THIS ALOUD IN UNISON.

God, we ask for vision. We ask for more than we could picture or imagine. We ask for wisdom and perception and a vision of where we're headed. We believe that You will give it to us, in some shape or form, and we believe that it will change the way we live, giving You all the glory.

UP NEXT

Leader, *before dismissing remind the group of what comes next.*

● Count the fruit of what God's done and write it down or share with someone.

_____

_____

_____

_____

_____

_____

● There are three days of personal study time to complete before we meet again.

● Read chapters 14–16 in the *You Are the Girl for the Job* book if you are following along.

MY PRAYER + YOUR PRAYER (10 MINUTES)

Each week ask a volunteer to read the short prayer for the group, *and* you will also write a short prayer for yourself. Where are you asking God to meet you this week? What are you hoping will happen?

> *God, get loud! We give You permission even though we know You don't need it! More than that, we beg in the name of Jesus that You'd eradicate anything that keeps us from hearing You clearly. We ask that You'd demolish pride and disbelief in our hearts as well as any defeat and discouragement. We ask that You'd help us to love the vision You pour out—even if we don't find ourselves on the stage, but rather in the shadows. Give us peace and passion and pursuit for Your kingdom as You speak to us clearly. We love you.*

Your turn:

_____

_____

_____

_____

_____

_____

_____

PERSONAL
STUDY

THOUGHTS FROM JESS

You may find that this week's individual study times are a little briefer than the ones we've previously covered. And that's intentional for one simple reason: there is a point of diminishing returns as it pertains to talking about hearing from God and hearing from God.

We can talk so much about hearing from God that we don't make time to hear from God and that's no good.

So my words may be more brief, but I pray you'll spend just as much (if not more!) time pouring out your devotion to Jesus. My hope is you'll spend that time with Him, hearing from Him and letting His vision, insight, and hope change your life.

This week we'll tear down some limiting beliefs about God, we'll dig into biblical knowledge that agrees with His character, and we'll hit the pavements—praying and communing and hearing from God as we go.

The enemy is scared, and he should be. A bunch of women are about to experience abundance.

DAY ONE:
HEART

Today we're going to go after three limiting beliefs with some truth to see if we can't sort our hearts out:

- God doesn't communicate with me the way He communicates with others.

- I'm worried I won't hear Him correctly, or that it's actually me that I'm hearing.

- I'm not sure He'll give me vision for what's to come.

Read **Isaiah 30:21** and rewrite it in the space below.

_____

_____

_____

_____

Specifically, this passage was written to the Israelites in the Old Testament, but do you notice any sort of qualifying characteristics that enable people to hear from God? List those characteristics here:

_____

_____

_____

Read Romans 8:38–39 and answer the following questions:

Will your past separate you from the love of God and thus His desire to communicate with you? **Yes/No**

Will your future separate you from the love of God and thus His desire to communicate with you? **Yes/No**

Will your intelligence separate you from the love of God and thus His desire to communicate with you? **Yes/No**

Will your capacity separate you from the love of God and thus His desire to communicate with you? **Yes/No**

Was it ever your goodness, your righteousness, or your character that united you with Christ in the first place? Define for yourself what unites you with Christ.

_____

_____

_____

_____

In what ways do your actions limit God's power and capacity to communicate with you or with anyone else He created and loves?

_____

_____

Read **Matthew 10:27** and rewrite it in the space below.

_____

_____

_____

For so many of us, fear about what God has told us comes in when it comes to telling others what we think He's communicated with us.

- The first piece of good news here is that I believe some of what God shares with us is just for us! Just for our intimacy and growth with Him! But, let's go back to Session 1 to remember another important truth ...

- Our goal in life is not to be right or to be the hero. If we make giving God glory our aim rather than being right ourselves, we'll live in some serious security.

Read 2 Timothy 3:16–17.

When you feel like God has told you something, describe what you should do to next.

_____

_____

Read **John 16:13** and rewrite it in the space below.

_____

_____

_____

_____

Do you believe God loves you? **Yes/No**

If your answer has changed, briefly acknowledge why or what the revelation was that changed your mind.

_____

_____

Do you believe God wants to give you insight into what's ahead? **Yes/No**

Claim your ability to receive God's insight for your life in an affirmation statement of truth.

_____

_____

_____

Do you still believe that maybe He withholds from you specifically? **Yes/No**

What are the barriers still holding you back? It's okay to have them, but you can't move past them until you can name them.

_____

_____

_____

Spend some time in prayer asking God to demolish any strongholds of doubt in your life before we move forward.

DAY TWO:
HEAD

Read Acts 9:1–19.

Who is God communicating with in this passage?

_____

What is His main message?

_____

Have you ever heard God specifically convict and correct your heart? In what way?

_____

_____

_____

Describe your response to the conviction.

_____

_____

How was that correction also a gift of vision?

_____

_____

Read Acts 8:26–40.

Who is God communicating with in this passage?

_____

_____

Describe the result of Philip's obedience to be available.

_____

_____

What would Philip have missed out on if he doubted the voice of the Holy Spirit?

_____

_____

Read Acts 10:9–48.

God is communicating with a handful of people in this passage. Who are they?

_____

There are two important and beautiful things happening in this passage I want you to capture:

1. What method is God using to help Peter understand what He's shown him?

_____

Right, other people! He's confirming this vision with the intimacy and communication He has with others. Which means many people's faith increases.

2. We see a countercultural decision being made based on this vision, but it lines up with the Word of God. Name it here: (Hint: Gentiles and baptism).

_____

Read Acts 1:8 and detail the kind of people with whom Jesus wanted His followers to share the gospel.

_____

_____

_____

Not only did Jesus heal Gentiles and minister to them while He was on earth, He commanded the gospel be preached to them and that they be baptized in His final words on earth.

So, while Peter's vision from God was countercultural, was it in line with the words of Jesus? **Yes/No**

Summarize whatever you notice and capture from reading these few passages of Scripture. What do you learn about God and how He communicates with His people.

_____

_____

_____

_____

DAY THREE:
HANDS

This week I want you to pick one or two of the following ideas and get with God. Be ready to report back to your group how your time with Him went.

☐ Go on a walk with God. Act as if He's right there with you (spoiler alert: He is!). Talk to Him and then record what you perceive He is saying back.

☐ Read the Word and ask Him to speak to you through it.

☐ Journal your thoughts as well as what you perceive God to be saying back to you.

☐ Pray for a dream from God.

☐ Gather some friends and spend time in prayer, talking to God and listening to Him also.

As always, check what you hear against the Word of God. Does it line up with His character? **Yes/No**

COUNT THE FRUIT

> *I am the vine; you are the branches. If you remain in me and I in you, you will bear much fruit; apart from me you can do nothing.*
>
> —John 15:5

Before you gather with your group again, take a moment to count the fruit. Here's what I mean by that: identify what God has grown in and through you this week.

God has accomplished _____ in me this week.

God has shown me _____.

God has answered my question(s) of _____.

God has reminded me of His capacity in this way this week:

_____

_____

_____

_____

God has shifted me, changed my mindset, altered my personal perspective in these ways:

_____

_____

_____

_____

> When we abide and remain in God's presence by praying, studying His Word, and even asking introspective questions, He grows us.

DAYS FOUR & FIVE
(OPTIONAL)

Read chapters 16–18 in the *You Are the Girl for the Job* book. **Reading through the book will enhance your experience of this study, but it is not required.**

6

BECAUSE GOD SAYS SO

SCHEDULE

Review this week's schedule as a group before opening your time together.

BEFORE THE GROUP MEETING	Read chapters 14–16 in *You Are the Girl for the Job* book
IN YOUR GROUP	• Set the Temperature (prayer) • Personal Heart Check-In • Watch the video teaching for Session 6 and take notes • Complete Discussion Questions • Change the Language/Change the Culture • My Prayer + Your Prayer
AT HOME	• Personal Study Day 1 (engage your heart with God's love) • Personal Study Day 2 (fill your head with God's truth) • Personal Study Day 3 (agree with abundance)

Stay in contact with the women who were part of this study. Live in abundance, in hope, and full confidence that YOU ARE THE GIRL FOR THE JOB!

GROUP STUDY

WELCOME NOTE FROM JESS (2 MINUTES)

Leader, *read note from Jess aloud to the group.*

I can't believe it's our last session together! I'm nothing but expectant, and I pray you are too.

What can God do with a group of women who are certain of His capacity in them? What can He does in the midst of a group of women committed to the good of others and the glory of God? What can He accomplish in a group of women who are not listening to the voice of fear but set on acting in faith—demolishing any idea that sets itself up against the knowledge of God? What might happen after we've partnered with the Holy Spirit to catch a vision for our lives that isn't about our fame but about His glory?

Beautiful things can happen. Beautiful things will happen.

We just get to make a move. So let's go.

SET THE TEMPERATURE (2 MINUTES)

Pick someone to open the group in prayer before we do our personal heart check.

Personal Heart Check (3 minutes)

Before we dig into this session's video, let's do a quick personal heart check. Take a minute or two to answer the following questions. You don't have to share these answers; this is just for you to pause and get honest with yourself and God.

A. On a scale of 1–10 (1 = very little, 10 = significantly), how much do you believe that God can change your life and change the world through you?

1   2   3   4   5   6   7   8   9   10

B. Do you feel ready to use what you've got for the good of others and the glory of God?

NO   A LITTLE SHAKY   DEFINITELY,
                  BUT CONFIDENT   WITH GOD'S HELP

C. How willing are you to be surprised by God for the rest of your life? (Circle, underline, or highlight how you feel this week.)

WON'T HAPPEN   THAT SOUNDS NICE   TEACH ME, CHANGE ME,
                                                    SURPRISE ME

VIDEO TEACHING (19 MINUTES)

Watch Video Session 6 and fill in the blanks throughout the teaching if you like:

- The starting line _____ _____ where you think it is.

- Less than shiny starting line people:

  _____ _____ _____

  _____ _____ _____

The JOB is this:

Live the abundant life God has crafted for you with intention, passion, and willingness to do whatever He's asked you to with a fine-tuned focus on His glory

- The starting line is with God . . . with His _____ and His _____ .

Take notes if you'd like:

Answer key: is not, Moses/Mary/Disciples/Rahab/Matthew/Paul/Peter, capacity/character

GROUP DISCUSSION (30 MINUTES)

Leader, *read each question aloud to the group. Take turns/volunteers for any Scripture reading.*

1. What did you think the starting line of mission, of living on purpose was supposed to look like?

2. What influenced your idea or concept of the starting line?

3. If your idea of the starting line has now changed since Jess' teaching, share in what ways. What has changed in your understanding of God in your life over the past five sessions that could contribute to a new understanding of your mission, that you ARE the girl for the job?

4. Is there anything still holding you back from something you know God has called you to be obedient to? Explain. Discuss as a group how to overcome any obstacles holding you back.

5. What do you think responding to this overall message will look like for you? Share with the group any hopes or dreams you have now for a life on mission with and for God, *or* if you are in the middle of experiencing your personal life on mission, has any part of your perception or response to that mission changed now? In what ways?

CHANGE THE LANGUAGE, CHANGE THE CULTURE (10 MINUTES)

When we change the language, we change the culture. When we put different words in our mouths, words that agree with God's character and capacity, things begin to shift not only in our lives but also in our communities.

Read Proverbs 18:21 aloud together.

Select one person to read a statement on the left, and then have another person read the alternate statement on the right. Talk about the difference you hear and feel in each change of the language. Discuss how these simple shifts in our language can effect change in our immediate culture. Commit to using language with one another that agrees with God's Word.

INSTEAD OF:	TRY THIS:
I can't do this.	God can do this.
I'm not ready yet.	God is equipping and empowering me.
She believed she could and so she did.	She believed He could, and she faithfully followed.
I'm a mess.	I am the girl for the job.

Let's ask God to help us watch all our language as it pertains to our strengths and our weaknesses. Is what we're saying biblical and true of His character? Are we speaking words that leave room for His redemption, His power, and His promises to take root?

READ THIS ALOUD IN UNISON.

God, You've placed us where we are, with what we have, on purpose, for the good of others and the fulfillment of Your glory. And if we believe You, believe in Your character and power, and take You at Your Word—we will change the world. We choose to believe!

UP NEXT

Leader, *before dismissing remind the group of what comes next.*

- Count the fruit of what God's done and write it down or share with someone.

_____

_____

_____

_____

_____

- There are three days of personal study time to complete before we meet again.

- Finish reading the book *You Are the Girl for the Job* if you haven't already.

- Tell five women in your life something you learned from this video Bible study.

- Review your answers to the Personal Heart Check each week and note the growth!

- Read each "Count the Fruit" section from Session 1 until now. Reflect on how great our God is and how very loved and cared for you are!

MY PRAYER + YOUR PRAYER (10 MINUTES)

Each week ask a volunteer to read the short prayer for the group, *and* you will also write a short prayer for yourself. Where are you asking God to meet you this week? What are you hoping will happen?

> *Father, we thank You for all You've done as we've look at Your truth and surrounded ourselves with Your women. We thank you for the fruit You've grown and the people You've shown us to love. We thank You for the gifts You've given and the weaknesses You've allowed and the fear You've*

defeated with Your power and Your love. We're Your girls—ready to be used by You, ready to obediently follow where You're leading. We love you. We're ready. Thank you for calling us and sending us. In Jesus' name, Amen.

Your turn:

_____

_____

_____

_____

_____

_____

_____

PERSONAL STUDY

FINAL THOUGHTS FROM JESS

I pray that at this point, the cuteness of the phrase "you are the girl for the job" has worn off and the power of this truth has sunk deep into your heart: *I am the girl for the job.*

I told you all at the beginning of this journey that the picture on the cover had to be a woman looking down at her own feet, where she stands, to declare this truth over her. It's great that I think you're the girl for the job, but it's wildly important that you believe that God has placed you where you are, on purpose, for the good of others and the glory of God.

I've talked occasionally about the enemy of our souls, but I want to speak plainly now: he wins the battle when we let feelings of inadequacy, fear, and indecision hold us back from obedience.

The enemy can't cause any pain in your life without getting permission from God, but he is the prince of this world—and he stirs strife among the generations to get them to discount themselves.

This needs to make us ANGRY. This needs to make us FRUSTRATED. And we need to stand firm, compelled by the grace of God, holding truth firmly in our grasp—ready to fight any pretense, any idea that sets itself up against the idea that our Father has placed us here on purpose for His glory and the good of others.

We have to fight with obedience and worship to believe that He will finish what He has started. This isn't just about our abundance but the life and the hope and the joy of all those He's sent us to love and minister to. Let's move forward with that sobering thought in our hearts. This is not just about us; this is war.

We won't be counted out by a dumb lying enemy who was already defeated by Christ's death on the cross. We won't be counted out by feelings of inadequacy when we know it's God's capacity that empowers us anyhow.

As you dig into the last few days of personal Bible study, let this message soak and be solidified in your heart.

DAY ONE:
HEART

Do you remember in our very first session when we described our ideal self and ask God to eradicate that picture from our minds? In what ways has your real self come alive in the past six weeks? Where are you still God's help to see through the ideal self and celebrate the real self?

_____

_____

_____

_____

Do you remember how we put to death the idea that we had to be put together to be used by Him? Have you done the heart work to really move past this idea? What has changed and what still might need to change?

_____

_____

_____

_____

_____

Today, I want you to do the opposite of the ideal-self-dreaming and just describe where you are right now, where He's placed you, what He's given you, and how mighty He is in you.

Spend some time journaling, describing the following:

What does life look like right now?

_____

_____

_____

_____

_____

Who has God give you to love and serve?

_____

_____

_____

_____

_____

What has God given you to work with —strengths and weaknesses?

_____

_____

_____

_____

What fears has He conquered in your life?

_____

_____

_____

_____

What vision has He given you?

_____

_____

_____

_____

How are you taking obedient steps forward?

_____

_____

_____

_____

_____

Flip back to Session 3 Day Two (pages 66–70) and use the Greek words, His Words, to write about yourself. As you describe your life, embrace the full strength of the Holy Spirit living within you!

_____

_____

_____

_____

> You are the girl for the job, and there's no need to wait for your ideal self to show up to tell this story. He is mighty, He is moving, and He is here.

DAY TWO:
HEAD

Read the following passages and find the unifying message that God gives. Note who God is talking to and what He tells them.

	WHO	WHAT
GENESIS 26:24		
JOSHUA 3:7		
ISAIAH 41:10		
JEREMIAH 1:8		
HAGGAI 1:13		
MATTHEW 28:20		
ACTS 18:10		

This one doesn't take rocket science nor does it take a lot of studying. You have one piece of head knowledge that can and should and will impact every act of obedience that you participate in for the rest of your life.

Who is with you?

_____

_____

_____

DAY THREE:
HANDS

You're ready for obedience, you have all you need because you have Jesus with you—working in and through you.

As you go, here are some practical tips:

TAKE A FRIEND

Read **Ecclesiastes 4:9–12**. Write it in the space below:

_____

_____

_____

_____

_____

_____

_____

_____

Who do you need to invite to go with you as you follow God in whatever He's calling you to?

_____

Maybe you don't need to ask someone to join you, but you need to ask them to pray with you, to remind you of truth and cheer you on. Share their names below, share when and how you're going to invite them into running together, and share how you plan on encouraging and spurring them on in their God-given calling.

_____

_____

_____

KEEP A RECORD

Read **Psalm 103:2**. Write it in the space below:

_____

_____

_____

_____

As you move forward obediently and worshipfully in what God has called you to, it will help so much if you continually count the fruit of what God has done and is doing in your mission.

Even if it seems small or insignificant, keep a record of how and when you see His hand move. Then you can look back on it and be encouraged in harder days.

Describe what this will look like for you. Will you keep a journal? Write a blog? Take pictures? Keep a list?

_____

_____

_____

WORSHIP AS YOU GO

Read **Psalm 95:6**. Write it in the space below:

_____

_____

_____

_____

Lastly, don't forget to worship, even as you run on mission using what you have for His glory and the good of others.

Connecting with God is still wildly important, even in the midst of using your gifts.

Strategize right now what kind of worship is most life-giving for you: is it through song, prayer, moving your body, or even rest?

Whatever it is, take it too far. Helping others connect with Him is beautiful, but you have to keep taking your place in the throne room of grace as well.

You're ready for this. And there are healthy and beautiful ways to move forward in obedience, keeping you in the grip of God's grace and receiving His mercy.

COUNT THE FRUIT

I am the vine; you are the branches. If you remain in me and I in you, you will bear much fruit; apart from me you can do nothing.

—John 15:5

Before you gather with your group again, take a moment to count the fruit. Here's what I mean by that: identify what God has grown in and through you this week.

God has accomplished _____ in me this week.

God has shown me _____.

God has answered my question(s) of _____.

God has reminded me of His capacity in this way this week:

_____

_____

_____

_____

God has shifted me, changed my mindset, altered my personal perspective in these ways:

_____

_____

_____

_____

> When we abide and remain in God's presence by praying, studying His Word, and even asking introspective questions, He grows us.

Stay in contact with the women who were part of this video Bible study. Live in abundance, in hope, and full confidence that YOU ARE THE GIRL FOR THE JOB!

God bless you wherever you are and wherever you are headed. Thank you from the bottom of my heart for joining me in this study of God's Word and the truth about who we are and what our purpose is!

You Are the Girl for the Job

Daring to Believe the God Who Calls You

Jess Connolly

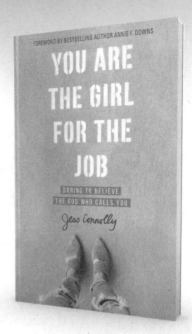

You believe (or want to believe) God has called you and given you purpose, but where do you start? How do you get from feeling stuck to making a move? If this sounds familiar, bestselling author Jess Connolly has a message for you: *You Are the Girl for the Job.*

But this is not simply a peppy catchphrase. This is the straight-up truth God has proclaimed over your life from the beginning, and it's not dependent on what you can do or achieve but based on His power, capacity, and character.

It has taken one million, maybe one zillion (who knows?!) slight moves of His hand to place you in this exact moment. So forget about fear and second-guessing your gifts, because God has meticulously prepared you to be an ambassador for the kingdom right where you are, here and now. Life is too short to get stuck in a holding pattern of shame, self-doubt, and comparison. So let this book be your very good news: you don't have to wait for permission when you've already been commissioned.

With passion and heart-pumping hope, Jess shows that being the girl for the job doesn't depend on your capacity. Rather, it has everything to do with God's capacity and our willingness. It has everything to do with believing we are who God says we are and quieting any inferior word spoken against us. Are you ready?

Let this book be your jumpstart into confident, purposed living, as Jess walks you through the six steps she has used to coach and encourage women for years: set your focus, take stock of the story that has shaped you, face your fear, catch the vision, make a plan, and finally, make your move—all in the bold belief that God has called you to every step of the journey.

Available in stores and online!

Also Available from Jess Connolly

Dance, Stand, Run is an invitation to the daughters of God to step into the movements of abundant life: dancing in grace, standing firm in holiness, and running on mission. Through story and study, Jess casts a fresh vision for how to live into your identity as a holy daughter of God, how to break free of cheap grace and empty rule-keeping, and finally, how to live out your holy influence with confidence before a watching world. Spoiler alert: it's a beautiful thing.

For anyone longing to take their place in what God is doing in the world, *Dance, Stand, Run* will rally your strength, refresh your purpose, and energize your faith in a God who calls us to be like Him.

Book
9780310345640

Study Guide
9780310090212

DVD
9780310090236

Available now at your favorite bookstore,
or streaming video on StudyGateway.com.

BIBLE STUDY
SOURCE
for women
powered by ChurchSource

Connecting you with the best in

BIBLE STUDY RESOURCES

from many of the world's

MOST TRUSTED BIBLE TEACHERS

JESS
CONNOLLY

JENNIE
ALLEN

JADA
EDWARDS

SHAUNA
NIEQUIST

Providing

WOMEN'S MINISTRY LEADERS,
SMALL GROUP LEADERS, AND INDIVIDUALS

with the

INSPIRATION, ENCOURAGEMENT, AND RESOURCES

every woman needs to grow their faith in every season of life

powered by ChurchSource

join our
COMMUNITY

Use our BIBLE STUDY FINDER to quickly find the perfect study for your group,
learn more about all the new studies available, and download FREE printables
to help you make the most of your Bible study experience.

BibleStudySourceForWomen.com

FIND THE *perfect* BIBLE STUDY
for you and your group in 5 MINUTES or LESS!

Find the right study for your women's group
by answering four easy questions:

1. WHAT TYPE OF STUDY DO YOU WANT TO DO?

- *Book of the Bible:* Dive deep into the study of a Bible character, or go through a complete book of the Bible systematically, or add tools to your Bible study methods toolkit.

- *Topical Issues:* Have a need in a specific area of life? Study the Scriptures that pertain to that need. Topics include prayer, joy, purpose, balance, identity in Christ, and more.

2. WHAT LEVEL OF TIME COMMITMENT BETWEEN SESSIONS WOULD YOU LIKE?

- *None:* No personal homework
- *Minimal:* Less than 30 minutes of homework
- *Moderate:* 30 minutes to one hour of homework
- *Substantial:* An hour or more of homework

3. WHAT IS YOUR GROUP'S BIBLE KNOWLEDGE?

- *Beginner:* Group is comprised mostly of women who are new to the Bible or who don't feel confident in their Bible knowledge.

- *Intermediate:* Group has some experience with studying the Bible, and they have some familiarity with the stories in the Bible.

- *Advanced:* Group is comfortable with the Bible, and can handle the challenge of searching the Scriptures for themselves.

4. WHAT FORMAT DO YOU PREFER?

- *Print and Video:* Watch a Bible teacher on video, followed by a facilitated discussion.

- *Print Only:* Have the group leader give a short talk and lead a discussion of a study guide or a book.

Get Started! Plug your answers into the **Bible Study Finder**, and discover the studies that best fit your group!

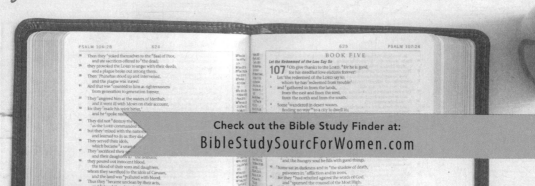

Check out the Bible Study Finder at:
BibleStudySourceForWomen.com